ZOO WORLD

THE VISIT OF TWO

GIANT PANDAS

AT THE SAN DIEGO ZOO

BY GEORGEANNE IRVINE

SIMON & SCHUSTER BOOKS FOR YOUNG READERS
Published by Simon & Schuster
New York · London · Toronto · Sydney · Tokyo · Singapore

To Basi and Yuan Yuan, whose visit changed my life forever, and to Mr. Chen, Xiao Ling and Mei Lin with love and friendship from Bamboo Shoot.

ACKNOWLEDGMENTS
Thank you to all of the San Diego Zoo employees who made the giant pandas' stay spectacular and successful, and to Alan Benjamin, Ron Garrison, Mabel Lam, Linda Dobbins, Dorothy Irvine, Victoria Garrison, Clayton Swanson, Kathi Diamant and Byron LaDue for helping me recreate their story. Also, my deep appreciation goes to Debbie Tabart, Terry Gorton and Mark Maglio for believing in my Gordy Foundation.

PHOTO CREDITS
Ron Garrison: front and back covers; endsheets; 5; 9; 10; 11; 12; 13; 15; 16; 17; 18; 19; 20; 21; 22; 24; 25; 26; 27; 28; 29; 30; 31; 33; 37; 38 left; 39; 40; 41; 43; 44. Craig Racicot: 23; 32; 42. Chen Yu Cun: 6; 35; 36. Georgeanne Irvine: 14; 38 right. Linda Dobbins: 34.

SIMON & SCHUSTER
BOOKS FOR YOUNG READERS
Simon & Schuster Building
Rockefeller Center
1230 Avenue of the Americas
New York, New York 10020
Copyright © 1991 by the Zoological Society
of San Diego and Georgeanne Irvine
SIMON & SCHUSTER BOOKS FOR YOUNG READERS
is a trademark of Simon & Schuster.
Designed by Kathleen Westray
Manufactured in the United States of America
10 9 8 7 6 5 4 3 2 1

Library of Congress Cataloging-in-Publication Data
Irvine, Georgeanne.
The visit of two giant pandas at the San Diego Zoo /
by Georgeanne Irvine.
p.   cm.
Summary: Relates the story of Basi and Yuan Yuan, two giant pandas from China who visited the San Diego Zoo as goodwill ambassadors to help Americans learn about the plight of their species.
1. Pandas—California—San Diego—Juvenile literature.   2. Basi (Panda)—Juvenile literature.   3. Yuan Yuan (Panda)—Juvenile literature.   4. San Diego Zoo—Juvenile literature.   [1. Basi (Panda) 2. Yuan Yuan (Panda)   3. Pandas.   4. San Diego Zoo.]   I. Title.
QL737.C214I78   1991
599.74'443—dc20   90-26235   CIP   AC
ISBN 0-671-73922-0

HIGH IN THE RUGGED Qionglai Mountains of central China, a young farm worker raced across the potato fields toward home. "I've found a giant panda that is starving!" she excitedly told her family and the other farm workers as she arrived at the village.

The people felt compelled to help the suffering animal. Giant pandas are an unusual and rare bear species, native only to China's interior mountain ranges. Even one death would be a great loss to the species' survival.

The peasants dropped what they were doing to organize a giant panda rescue patrol. They grabbed a large cage, some rope, and a long pole, then followed the young woman back across the fields and into a forest thick with towering fir, spruce, and maple trees. They crossed a raging stream and entered Basi Gou (Basi Gully), which was covered with dingy yellow patches of dead bamboo as far as they could see.

Near the bamboo and partly submerged in the stream lay a young giant panda, barely alive. The farm worker and villagers quickly pulled the animal from the water and gently dried it with their jackets. The dull eyes of the panda gazed up at the girl as it panted for breath.

Several other rescuers lifted the panda into the cage. The long pole was tied to the top of the cage to make it easy for the villagers to carry the panda out of the forest. Two men—one at each end—balanced the pole on their shoulders so that the caged panda dangled between them. They hiked down the mountain to a Baoxing County giant panda rescue station that had been set up by the Chinese government. There, the starving panda, a female that was named Basi after the gully in which she was found, was nursed back to health.

Basi was starving because in 1983, the year before she was rescued, the bamboo died in Baoxing County and in other regions of the Qionglai Mountains. Bamboo leaves, shoots, and stalks are the giant pandas' main food. Although they will also eat meat, pandas are usually too slow to catch the rats, squirrels, and other small mammals that share their forest habitat.

It is normal for bamboo to die every forty to one hundred years. Before it dies, the bamboo, which is really a woody grass, flowers and drops seeds so new bamboo can sprout. Several years must pass, though, before the seeds grow into tall new bamboo plants that the giant pandas can eat.

Years ago, when the bamboo died in one area,

the giant pandas could travel easily to a different mountain to find more living bamboo. But now, new farms and villages often block their way, so many pandas simply starve to death in withered bamboo patches. Then, too, many forests and bamboo thickets have been destroyed to build these farms and villages.

The villagers were pleased that they had saved Basi's life. Giant pandas are considered a national treasure of the People's Republic of China...and they are a critically endangered species.

To think that there are now only about seven hundred of one of the world's most popular animals alive in their misty mountain homes is frightening. There are so few giant pandas because of habitat destruction, periodic bamboo die-offs, and poaching. Amazingly, even though it is illegal, people still kill pandas for their pelts, which they sell for up to a hundred thousand dollars apiece. In addition, other animals that share the giant pandas' habitat—such as raccoon-like lesser pandas, golden monkeys, and leopards —are also becoming scarcer.

The Chinese government is doing a great deal to save the big black-and-white bears that are known as the clowns of the bamboo forests. Twelve nature reserves—protected areas where the pandas can live—have been established. Anti-poaching units patrol the reserves to guard the giant pandas against poachers and to destroy their traps. Trees and bamboo are being planted in corridors to link panda habitats together. This way, the giant pandas can bypass the farms and villages that block their way from one mountain to another.

Scientists are studying giant pandas in some reserves to learn as much about the animals and their behavior as possible. They use radio-tracking equipment and can follow the animals through their daily routines. The scientists sometimes

Pekin robins

Francois' leaf monkey

relocate giant pandas from one area to another to disperse the population more evenly. This is done to make sure there is enough food for the pandas and enough males and females near each other to produce cubs.

Whenever the bamboo dies, organized giant panda patrols search for starving pandas to give them food or to take them to rescue stations where they can recover. Some recent studies in India have resulted in what many researchers claim to be a scientific breakthrough in understanding the flowering cycle of bamboo. In the future, scientists may be able to control the bamboo die-offs in China, which in turn will save the lives of many giant pandas.

Nature reserves and zoos in China are breeding giant pandas in captivity to help make sure the species will not become extinct. The few other zoos around the world that have their own giant pandas are trying to breed them, as well. Although Ling-Ling and Hsing-Hsing, the National Zoo's giant pandas in Washington, D.C., have become parents several times, the zoo has had great difficulty keeping the cubs alive.

After Basi regained her strength at the giant panda rescue station, it was decided that she

golden monkey

dhole

would not be returned to the Qionglai Mountains. Instead, her new home would be the Fuzhou Zoo in southeastern China. There, Basi could be part of an important panda conservation and breeding program as soon as she was old enough to have cubs. The Fuzhou Zoo is well-known for its work with giant pandas, and one of its pandas, Qing Qing, has become a mother several times.

About the same time Basi was taken to the Fuzhou Zoo, a young male arrived there, too. Like Basi, he was rescued by a panda patrol during the bamboo die-off in the Qionglai Mountains. He was named Yuan Yuan after

Yuantuo Shan (Round Head Hill), the area where he was found starving.

In 1987, the Chinese government chose Basi and Yuan Yuan to do something very special that would help giant pandas all over China. They were selected to go to the United States for two hundred days as goodwill ambassadors to help Americans learn about the plight of the giant panda. Money raised by their visit would be donated to help China save giant pandas and other endangered species.

The lucky zoo chosen to host Basi and Yuan Yuan was the world-famous San Diego Zoo in

California. Since 1979, the San Diego Zoo has had a very friendly relationship with the People's Republic of China. The San Diego Zoo has given many rare animals to Chinese zoos, including African elephants, orangutans, rhinoceroses, and Amazon parrots. In return, San Diego has received dozens of Chinese animal species like Francois' leaf monkeys, Sichuan takins, Pekin robins, Manchurian brown bears, bharals (blue sheep), dholes (wild dogs), red-crowned cranes, and monal pheasants. The Chinese government even loaned the San Diego Zoo an incredibly rare and treasured animal species, the blue-faced golden monkey, which had never before been exhibited outside of China. The friendship between the San Diego Zoo and China has grown stronger because they are working together to save endangered species.

When San Diego Zoo officials heard that Basi and Yuan Yuan were coming to visit in July of 1987, the excitement began. Giant pandas had never been in San Diego before. The world's most famous zoo would be home for a while to a pair of one of the world's most popular animals.

HISTORY WAS ABOUT to be made for the San Diego Zoo. United Airlines Flight 90, direct from China, would be landing at any moment at Los Angeles International Airport. Riding in the airplane's cargo compartment were two giant panda passengers that the zoo had been hoping to host for years.

A bundle of fresh bamboo and a carton of crisp apples lay side by side on the dock of the United Airlines cargo terminal. A security guard stood watch nearby, guarding the leafy green stalks and the shiny red fruit as if they were gold. Basi and Yuan Yuan, the giant pandas from China's Fuzhou Zoo, might crave a snack, and bamboo and apples were their favorite treats. The two pandas were probably the most unusual travelers that the pilot had ever flown on his 747 jet, which had been nicknamed the San Diego Zoo Panda Express for the occasion.

The media were out in force because any giant

panda visit to the United States is a major news event. Americans love the comical black-and-white bears that turn somersaults and stand on their heads when they play.

Over fifty reporters and photographers waited eagerly with San Diego Zoo officials aboard an airport bus that was parked where the huge red-, blue-, and orange-striped plane would pull up to gate 122. The group clapped and cheered as the United Airlines jet touched down a few minutes after noon on a hot summer day. Seventeen hours had passed since the airliner had left China.

Everyone waited breathlessly as Flight 90's cargo hatch opened. Basi and Yuan Yuan had traveled in their own private compartment, complete with heating and air conditioning. The photographers leaped off the bus and raced toward the jet. High above the clicking cameras sat Basi and Yuan Yuan in their travel cages, peering down at the excited, grinning crowd. The giant pandas were here...at last!

As a special elevator lowered the pandas to the ground, Yuan Yuan sniffed the air and Basi laid back to munch on a mouthful of bamboo leaves. It had been a calm, comfortable flight, and both pandas seemed relaxed.

Basi's and Yuan Yuan's Fuzhou Zoo caretakers had arrived on Flight 90, too, only they rode in the passenger section. Yuan Yuan's keeper was Mei Lin, a nineteen-year-old Chinese woman; twenty-year-old Xiao Ling cared for Basi. In charge of the keepers and their pandas was the Fuzhou Zoo director and veterinarian, Mr. Chen. With permission from United Airlines and the U.S. Customs Department, the three people joined Basi and Yuan Yuan at planeside to escort them by tram back to the cargo terminal.

At the cargo terminal, there was even more excitement and activity. It was as if a king and queen had arrived. A red-and-white banner read UNITED AIRLINES WELCOMES BASI AND YUAN YUAN. Of course, giant pandas can't read; but an interpreter translated it for Mr. Chen and the panda keepers. They smiled, nodded their heads, and felt very welcomed to America.

While many important people gave speeches, more cameras clicked at Basi and Yuan Yuan. What mattered most to the VIP pandas, though, were the shiny red apples and the leafy green bamboo stalks that were waiting for them.

Basi sat curled up in her cage with a crisp apple in her paw. She held it like a human holds an apple because giant pandas have an extra-long wristbone that they use like a thumb. No other bear can grasp things as tightly as a giant panda. Like a well-mannered young lady, Basi took one small bite of the juicy apple at a time. She chewed very slowly, bite after bite, until all that was left was the stem. Then she ate that, too.

Yuan Yuan munched quietly on apples and bamboo, carefully licking the leftover bits off his mouth. Sometimes he stretched his furry black paw far out of the cage to try to tap people as they walked by.

Finally, a rumbling forklift hoisted Basi and Yuan Yuan, cages and all, into a Panda Express truck for the ride south to San Diego. Two black-and-white highway patrol cars escorted the two black-and-white bears all the way to the zoo.

As the Panda Express rolled through the back gate of the zoo, a huge crowd was gathering at the new Panda Plaza, a $1\frac{1}{2}$-acre exhibit where Basi and Yuan Yuan would live during their stay. Mr. Chen and the panda keepers were to live there, too, because they wanted to be near their animals at all times. Even though Panda Plaza was still closed to the public, about seventy-five excited zoo employees, plus more reporters and photographers, waited to greet the furry Chinese visitors.

Construction workers scurried around, too, because Panda Plaza wasn't finished yet. Basi's and Yuan Yuan's sleeping quarters were finished; and the trailers for Mr. Chen, Xiao Ling, and Mei Lin were in place behind a fence. However, there was still lots of sawing, hammering, and painting to be done to get the exhibit spruced up for the grand opening only four days away.

The zoo employees clapped and cheered as the Panda Express truck backed up to the plaza. Even the busy construction crew stopped work for a moment to watch as Basi and Yuan Yuan were unloaded from the truck.

Keeper Mei Lin brushed Yuan Yuan a bit before wheeling his cage toward the indoor panda bedroom area where he would sleep at night. A TV reporter squatted right in front of Yuan Yuan to do a live television story. Yuan Yuan turned his back to the camera, which made everyone laugh, even the reporter.

As Basi's cage rolled past the crowd, she snacked on yet another apple. Both Basi and Yuan Yuan probably could have eaten apples and bamboo for the rest of the day, but they needed a bath before they were released into their clean new bedrooms for the night.

19

When a cool stream of water from a green garden hose splashed Basi, she sneezed, snorted, and swiped at the shower. After Xiao Ling had scrubbed the sudsy panda clean with a long-handled brush, Basi shook her soggy, shaggy body and sent water flying everywhere.

Keeper Mei Lin spoke softly to Yuan Yuan as she shampooed his hind end and powder-puff tail. He wiggled and twitched when the brush touched his stomach because he was ticklish. As Mei Lin rinsed Yuan Yuan with a sprinkle and a spray, he bowed his head until his chin rested on his chest while rubbing his tiny black ears with his paws. He breathed in deeply, and then showered Mei Lin as he shook himself dry.

Watching Xiao Ling and Mei Lin work with Basi and Yuan Yuan, it was obvious that the young Chinese women had a special relationship with their animals. There was a definite bond between them. Even though pandas are wild animals, Basi and Yuan Yuan seemed to like the human contact; and they weren't bothered by the big fuss that was being made over them.

Mr. Chen and the panda keepers inspected

the panda exhibit and bedrooms to make sure everything was just right. Basi and Yuan Yuan had separate bedrooms. In the wild, giant pandas live by themselves and only get together to breed, so Mr. Chen felt they should be kept apart most of the time. Too much time together might cause a squabble between them.

Their exhibits were separate, too; but if they felt friendly, they could rub noses or touch paws through the bars that divided them. The enclosures were air-conditioned in case the temperature soared above seventy-five degrees. In China, wild pandas live at such high elevations that the temperature is usually chilly. At the zoo, cool air came out of ducts hidden in gigantic cement boulders surrounded by clumps of birch trees.

There was one major problem with Basi's pen though. A big pond had been built right in the middle of it. Mr. Chen felt Basi needed more room to move around, so the pond had to go. Besides, Mr. Chen said that Basi preferred showers to swimming in a pool.

Workers with jackhammers came to tear out the panda pond—and what a racket they made! A cement truck as tall as a house roared into Panda Plaza to fill up the hole with concrete. Still tired from their long journey, Basi and Yuan Yuan snoozed through all the noise.

Early Monday morning, a few days after Basi and Yuan Yuan arrived, zoo roosters crowed, peacocks cackled, kookaburras giggled, and a mist rose from the hippos' pond. People were already lining up at the main entrance to the zoo. Today was giant panda premiere day!

Eight hundred special friends of the San Diego Zoo, who had received invitations to be the first to see the giant pandas, crowded into Panda Plaza. Soothing Chinese music played softly, but the guests were very animated. They couldn't wait to meet Basi and Yuan Yuan.

With the sharp crack of a drum and the clanging of cymbals, a traditional Chinese lion dance began the festivities. Dancers in a colorful, shimmery lion costume swooped and swirled in front of Panda Plaza. The enormous head bobbed and bounced as the lion's sparkling eyes fluttered open and shut.

Young children marched by, waving pink, blue, green, and yellow flags. Mrs. Williams, the president of the Zoological Society of San Diego, and several Chinese dignitaries spoke of the friendship and goodwill that giant pandas bring

wherever they go. They called pandas a good-luck symbol of China and said they hoped they would bring good luck and happiness to San Diego.

With two clangs of a Chinese gong, bamboo curtains covering the front of the enclosures were rolled up. The pens were empty. Where were Basi and Yuan Yuan?

After a few moments, out waddled Yuan Yuan with keeper Mei Lin. The crowd gasped at its first sight of this extraordinary animal.

Mei Lin coaxed Yuan Yuan over to a boulder, where he promptly flopped down. He leaned his back against the rock so that he faced the hundreds of visitors. After a pawshake with Yuan Yuan, Mei Lin dropped a bunch of plump red grapes into his furry palm. He sat cradling the grapes in both paws, plucking and eating one grape at a time with his massive mouth. When a single grape fell off the stem and rolled down his belly, Yuan Yuan gently picked up the tiny fruit and popped it in his mouth. Before Mei Lin left the enclosure, she set down a bowl of pears and apples for the hungry panda.

The crowd was so enchanted with Yuan Yuan and Mei Lin that they barely noticed Xiao Ling setting up a folding chair and other props in

Basi's enclosure. Then, as lively Chinese music played over the loudspeakers, out ambled Basi with Xiao Ling at her side.

Xiao Ling pointed a short wand at the chair, and Basi climbed up and straddled the seat. Xiao Ling rewarded her with a bit of special panda bread made of rice, wheat, soybeans, and corn. While Xiao Ling fastened a collar around Basi's neck, the gentle animal looked all around, sniffing the air with her shiny black nose.

When Xiao Ling waved the wand again, Basi crawled off the chair, stood on her hind legs, and shuffled across her pen. When her keeper handed her a bouquet of colorful flowers, Basi waved them at the crowd. Besides being well-behaved like Yuan Yuan, Basi was a performer, and the crowd loved it.

Basi's next feat was to push a stroller across the floor. Basi had trouble steering the stroller, so Xiao Ling helped her guide it.

Whenever Xiao Ling spoke to Basi (in Chinese, of course), the trained panda knew just what to do. When Xiao Ling handed Basi a human baby doll, the panda cradled it in her arms and gently patted it on the back. Next, Xiao Ling gave Basi a plastic bottle. Back and forth, back and forth Basi's head turned, first licking the bottle and then licking the baby. People oohed and aahed, and everyone hoped Basi would herself become a mother to a baby panda one day.

Most certainly Basi would care for her own baby a bit differently. A giant panda cub is born blind (its eyes are closed until it is forty days old) and helpless. Its pink body is covered with thin, white hair that doesn't begin to thicken and turn black in spots until it is a week old. The newborn panda weighs about 4 ounces (the weight of a stick of butter) and is eight hundred times smaller than its mother. To protect her infant and to keep it warm during its first month of life, the mother panda holds it in one furry paw, cradling it against her body. Her cub's loud cries are a signal that it is hungry. The mother holds her infant to her breast up to fourteen times a day so it can suckle her milk. As the baby grows bigger and stronger, it nurses less often. The mother will leave an older cub alone in a den, while she feeds on bamboo.

26

Before waving good-bye to the guests, Basi entertained them with one more feat. She caught a baton that Xiao Ling tossed to her, twirling it round and round with both paws like a majorette leading a parade.

With thundering applause from the crowd, the panda premiere and Basi's first daily performance ended. Basi was then treated to a feast of bamboo and apples, and was soon sound asleep.

When the main gate of the zoo opened to the public, thousands of panda fans streamed through the turnstiles. They raced right past a flock of brilliant pink flamingos, a cuddly-looking koala, and a pair of shaggy two-humped camels straight to Basi and Yuan Yuan's exhibit. They followed bright red banners along the way. Throughout the giant pandas' stay in San Diego, that path to their zoo home was very well traveled.

A narrator stationed next to Basi's and Yuan Yuan's enclosures explained many facts about giant pandas to the crowds. Besides discussing panda conservation, she told the visitors that, until recently, most people had disagreed about what kind of animal a giant panda really is. Some scientists thought giant pandas were related to raccoons. Others believed they were in an animal family of their own that included a small

raccoonlike animal called a lesser panda. But now, she explained, scientists have studied the chromosomes of giant pandas, and most agree they are bears.

The narrator said that the giant pandas' powerful jaws and wide, flat back teeth are specially adapted for crushing and chewing bamboo stalks. Bamboo is so tough that even a person using a hatchet has trouble cutting through the stalk, yet giant pandas can easily tear it apart.

People were amazed to learn that each Fuzhou panda ate about 22 pounds of bamboo a day in addition to their fruit and panda bread. In the

wild, a panda might eat up to 40 pounds of bamboo daily. Giant pandas eat so much because they have trouble digesting their food. Their intestines are short, so meals pass through their bodies quickly. The only way for a giant panda to nourish itself is to consume huge quantities of food.

Although most visitors never heard Basi and Yuan Yuan vocalizing, the narrator said that giant pandas can communicate using eleven different sounds—snorts, growls, roars, huffs, bleats, barks, moans, chirps, squeals, honks, and squawks.

Soon Basi became famous all over the United States for what Mr. Chen and the keepers called her "exercise sessions." Not only could she twirl a baton and burp a baby doll, but she was great at dribbling a basketball and slam-dunking it through a hoop. Basi lifted barbells, rode a rocking horse, and delicately balanced on a teeterboard while she caught rings on her mittenlike paws. She could even lie on her back and roll a red-, green-, and yellow-striped barrel on all four feet. And, for the fun of it, Xiao Ling sometimes pretended Basi was in the Olympics, and hung a medal around her neck and gave her a trophy.

Yuan Yuan could walk on his hind legs, sit on a chair, hold a basketball, and wave. Because he

was still learning, he never performed for the public; but he practiced with Mei Lin every night when visitors weren't around.

Basi and Yuan Yuan weren't being trained just to be entertaining. There were important reasons for them to learn and perfect their motor skills.

If the Fuzhou Zoo pandas had remained in the wild, they would have been active for up to 14 hours a day. Most of that time would have been spent collecting and eating food in the mountain forests; but some of it would have been used for play—climbing stumps, trees, and boulders, and rolling down hillsides. In captivity, Basi's and Yuan Yuan's routines were an excellent way for them to stay active, coordinated, and healthy.

Important, too, was the close bond that had developed between the giant pandas and their trainers, Xiao Ling and Mei Lin. These trusting relationships were critical to Mr. Chen's plans for the panda conservation program. Mr. Chen hoped that in the future, when Basi gave birth, she would let Mr. Chen get close enough to the cub to examine it and make sure it was healthy.

Because Basi and Yuan Yuan were so used to human contact, they already allowed Mr. Chen to give them medical exams while they were wide awake. Usually, giant pandas must be put to sleep with tranquilizers before a veterinarian can even get near them. Mr. Chen made house calls right to the pandas' enclosures, and Xiao Ling and Mei Lin helped him handle the animals and gather data for medical records.

Weighing Basi and Yuan Yuan was easy. The young women coaxed each animal on to a large, flat electronic scale. Basi usually sat or stood calmly while her weight was read, but Yuan Yuan would sometimes get playful and try to scoot off the scale. Mei Lin scolded him when he did this but always rewarded him with panda bread when he sat still. When a weigh-in session was over, 220-pound Yuan Yuan often turned somersaults off the scale.

Basi, who weighed about 200 pounds, and Yuan Yuan were of normal size. Giant pandas usually weigh between 175 and 275 pounds.

For the rest of their physical examination, Basi and Yuan Yuan either lay on the ground or sat in folding chairs. Mr. Chen listened to the pandas' hearts, took their temperatures, and measured their blood pressures and breathing rates. He could even give the animals shots if they were sick, or collect blood samples. Basi and Yuan

Yuan always munched on apples and panda bread during their exam, and Mr. Chen always remembered to shake their paws when he was done.

The medical data Mr. Chen collected would be helpful to other scientists who were trying to save the giant panda species from extinction. These scientists needed to know as much about pandas and their bodies as possible. Because Basi and Yuan Yuan weren't tranquilized with drugs when they were examined, such readings as heart and breathing rates and body temperatures were

more accurate. So by allowing Mr. Chen to give them medical exams, Basi and Yuan Yuan were helping giant pandas everywhere.

Although Basi and Yuan Yuan were well-behaved giant pandas, Mr. Chen, Xiao Ling, and Mei Lin had to remember that they were still wild animals. The Fuzhou Zoo keepers were very careful when they worked with Basi and Yuan Yuan because giant pandas could certainly be unfriendly or mischievous at times.

Yuan Yuan usually was rowdier than Basi, and because he didn't have as much training as Basi, the keepers normally were more cautious with him.

Poor Mei Lin learned an important lesson one evening as she was bathing Yuan Yuan in his behind-the-scenes bedroom. As usual, she lathered and scrubbed him well, and then rinsed him off with a hose. He romped around the room while he shook himself dry. As Mei Lin headed for the door, she turned her back on Yuan Yuan for only a few seconds, but it was too late. Yuan Yuan bit her on the back of the leg. He wasn't being nasty, just playful. It was a painful reminder to Mei Lin that she must always keep her eyes on Yuan Yuan.

Baths often put the giant pandas in a lively mood. After a cool morning shower, the bears

would often amuse zoo visitors with spirited wrestling matches carried on through the bars between their pens. Yuan Yuan would stand on his hind legs to bat at Basi. Then he would run away and somersault a couple of times. When he came back, Basi would grab his ears or bop him on his nose. He might play-bite her on the shoulder before twirling around on his bottom like a spinning top. A few more smacks here and a few more whacks there usually ended the round. But sometimes there was more, perhaps a bamboo tug-of-war.

Yuan Yuan would tease Basi with his leafy bamboo stalks. She had her own bamboo, but Yuan Yuan's seemed to look more appetizing, especially when he dragged it over to the fence. With one giant panda reach through the bars, Basi easily grabbed Yuan Yuan's bamboo. He'd cling tightly to the other end. Back and forth, up and down they'd pull, until roly-poly Yuan Yuan would let go.

Some of the pandas' antics were more adventurous and sometimes more dangerous. Yuan Yuan was determined to climb the slender birch

trees in the back of his enclosure. On his first trip up one of these trees, he almost made it to the top. Just as the tree was bending over the exhibit wall, it broke and sent Yuan Yuan tumbling to the ground. If the tree hadn't cracked, he might have slipped out of his pen. Yuan Yuan eventually broke all of the other trees, too. He then discovered that the stumps were perfect panda back scratchers.

Basi managed to break out of her exhibit several times. This greatly concerned Mr. Chen, Xiao Ling, and Mei Lin.

One getaway was up and over the back wall of her enclosure. Clever Basi pushed a table against the wall that Xiao Ling left in the pen as a prop for her exercise sessions. Basi stood on the table and stretched until she reached the top of the wall. Then she easily dropped to the other side, where she settled herself down on a bushy bamboo hillside. After Xiao Ling lured the escape artist back to the exhibit with an apple, the prop table quickly was moved to a storage area.

Another escape surprised a lot of people who were visiting the giant pandas on a drizzly fall afternoon. One moment, Basi was ambling inside her enclosure; the next, she was strolling along the top of the wall that separated her from Yuan Yuan. Basi had managed this by discovering a foothold on a padlock that fastened a door between the two pens.

Visitors were fascinated that Basi was out, but zoo security guards and the panda keepers were concerned. They knew that if Basi became frightened, she might hurt someone. Basi balanced easily on the wall, just like a tightrope walker in a circus. She headed toward the crowd; but when everyone gasped, the giant panda changed directions and dropped in with Yuan Yuan.

Round and round Basi and Yuan Yuan rolled, play-biting each other until Mei Lin lured Yuan Yuan into his bedroom with an apple. Basi followed her panda playmate, but then Xiao Ling tossed another apple out of the bedroom and away from Yuan Yuan. Basi chose her favorite snack over more romping, and the two pandas were finally separated.

Mr. Chen was upset that Basi had escaped once more. He thought she would try to get out again. But she would never get the chance. The next day, construction workers raised the walls of both Basi's and Yuan Yuan's pens by adding 4-foot-high panes of Plexiglas™.

One good thing which came from Basi's last escape was that Mr. Chen decided to let Basi and Yuan Yuan play together from time to time. They were closely supervised by him and the panda keepers as they roughhoused with no bars between them.

During their stay in San Diego, Xiao Ling and Mei Lin spent most of their time caring for Basi and Yuan Yuan. They cleaned their pens, fixed their meals, bathed and exercised them, and checked up on the two throughout the day and night.

Even though the young women were very busy being giant panda keepers, they still had time to make some new friends in America. They learned a few words of English, but most of the time they still needed the interpreter to help them speak with their American friends.

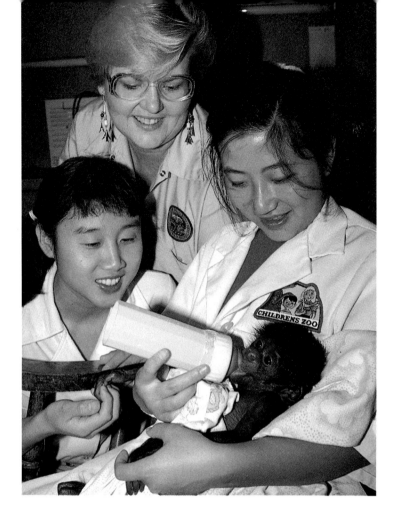

At the zoo, nursery attendant JoAnn Thomas-Roemer taught them all about Marilyn, an infant pygmy chimpanzee. The two learned that tiny Marilyn needed as much care as a human baby. Xiao Ling and Mei Lin would sometimes help JoAnn by diapering and feeding the little chimp, and by playing with her.

Other new friends showed Xiao Ling and Mei Lin the sights of Southern California. The panda keepers enjoyed the rides at Disneyland and met Mickey and Minnie Mouse, Donald Duck, and Winnie the Pooh. King Kong shook their tram at Universal Studios, while a wild roller coaster shook their stomachs at Knotts Berry Farm. At

a miniature golf course, Xiao Ling hit a hole in one, and in a game of bumper boats, Mei Lin managed to get everyone soaking wet.

It was fun for the Chinese visitors to explore shopping malls, and at times those trips resulted in new jeans for Xiao Ling or a blouse for Mei Lin. They especially enjoyed visiting American homes for dinner and for holidays like Thanksgiving and Christmas. Life and customs in the United States were very different from those in China.

During the Christmas season, Basi gave the San Diego Zoo visitors something more to smile about. In her exercise sessions, she charmed adults and children by cuddling a stuffed toy panda that wore a red-and-white Santa Claus hat. After showing off her Santa panda, she held up a giant-sized card that read SEASON'S GREETINGS FROM BASI AND YUAN YUAN. Holiday photographs of Basi ran in newspapers all over the world.

In mid-January of 1988, a month before Basi and Yuan Yuan were to go home to China, a violent storm hit Southern California. All through the night, thunder roared and heavy rain pummeled the San Diego Zoo. Even worse than the downpour was the wind that raged at 65 miles per hour.

Mr. Chen and the panda keepers were terrified. They rushed from their trailers to the safety of Basi's and Yuan Yuan's cement bedroom area. They hoped that the walls were strong enough to protect them and the pandas from any large trees that might hit Panda Plaza. Basi and Yuan Yuan were very nervous. They paced in their bedrooms and stood up on their hind legs, sniffing at the door as if that might tell them what all the racket was about. They also honked and squealed; these are sounds giant pandas make when they are distressed.

A few hours before dawn, the storm finally ended. The giant pandas and their caretakers were fine; but Mr. Chen, Xiao Ling, and Mei Lin worried about how the rest of the animals had fared. It was still too dark to see what damage had been done; and, in case some animals had escaped, it wasn't safe to be outside before day-light. Even though other keepers weren't due at the zoo until 6 A.M., they hurried to work as soon as the storm was over to check on their animals.

When the sun finally peeked out from behind leftover storm clouds, everyone was shocked at the damage. One-hundred-foot-tall eucalyptus trees had crashed down all around the zoo, blocking roads and smashing animal enclosure walls. At a show amphitheater right next to Panda Plaza, a half dozen towering trees had fallen on the twelve-hundred-person seating area, leaving it a shambles. The trees had just missed Basi's and Yuan Yuan's bedrooms!

Amazingly, no animals escaped or were injured during the storm. The zoo was closed to visitors for a day so workers could clean up the mess. What a story the panda caretakers could tell back in China! They had weathered what the zoo director proclaimed to be "the worst storm in the history of the San Diego Zoo."

As the time drew nearer for Basi and Yuan Yuan to travel back to Fuzhou, plans were made for their departure. People who had waited until the last minute to see the giant pandas now hurried to the zoo. Basi continued her performance several times a day, while Yuan Yuan clowned as usual. When the pandas weren't eating, playing, or exercising, they were napping.

Even sleeping giant pandas can be entertaining for the visitors. Basi used many things for pillows —her props, her paws, and her air-conditioned rocks. Most unusual was when Basi would lean against a rock, stick her left foot in the air, and then prop her chin on the foot while she napped. It was hard to understand how she didn't fall over.

Yuan Yuan liked to nap while stretched out on his belly or back on top of the cool air ducts in his rocks. He also slept hunched over or curled up like a doughnut.

41

On February 9, 1988, there were many sad faces at the zoo. It was Basi and Yuan Yuan's last day on exhibit. The lovable pair and their caretakers would leave for China the next day.

Saying good-bye was difficult because San Diego had fallen in love with Basi and Yuan Yuan. More than two million people from all over the world had come to see these famous giant pandas, and no one wanted to see them go.

At a farewell ceremony, the Zoological Society president, Mrs. Williams, spoke to guests and reporters again. "Basi and Yuan Yuan have been our teachers," she said. "They taught us that pandas are a Chinese wildlife treasure which we all must help protect and preserve. Our door will always be open to our new friends from China."

As Basi performed for the last time, Yuan Yuan munched on his favorite food, bamboo. When Basi burped her baby doll, rode her rocking horse, and balanced on her teeterboard, everyone clapped and cheered as always. But this time, tears glistened in many people's eyes. How attached they had become to these black-and-white visitors from China.

Just before Basi waved her final good-bye to her human friends, she held up a sign that Xiao Ling placed in her paws. It read BASI AND YUAN YUAN BID A FOND FAREWELL TO SAN DIEGO.

Their journey home began at 3 A.M. the next day, while Panda Plaza was still pitch dark. About two dozen zoo employees showed up to help load the Panda Express truck and to escort Basi, Yuan Yuan, and their caretakers back to Los Angeles International Airport. Although the United Airlines flight wasn't taking off until 11:25 A.M., the giant panda passengers had to be checked in many hours earlier than the human passengers.

Everyone tried to be cheerful, but inside they felt heavyhearted because their Chinese friends— both human and animal—were leaving. Mr. Chen, Xiao Ling, and Mei Lin were excited to be going home; but they, too, were sad to be saying good-bye to their new American friends.

At the United Airlines cargo terminal, there were many reporters and photographers, just as there had been when the pandas arrived. Basi and Yuan Yuan were showered once more by Mr. Chen to freshen them up for the long trip home. Pieces of plywood were wired to the sides of the pandas' cages to protect them during the flight.

The precious giant pandas that people had grown to love were carted by tram to the same United Airlines jet that had brought them to America. Xiao Ling and Mei Lin cried as they hugged their zoo friends good-bye. Mr. Chen smiled, bowed, then hugged his new friends, too.

Basi and Yuan Yuan were going home to China. Most likely, they would never return to the San Diego Zoo because it was time for Basi to become a mother and Yuan Yuan a father. But they had more than accomplished their mission.

For the millions who met them, the giant pandas from the Fuzhou Zoo were wildlife treasures to be cherished. Basi and Yuan Yuan had been splendid goodwill ambassadors, not only for giant pandas but for other endangered animals, as well.

BIBLIOGRAPHY

Barrett, Norman. *Picture Library: Pandas.* New York: Franklin Watts Ltd, 1988.

Belson, Jenny, and Gilheany, James. *The Giant Panda Book.* London: William Collins Sons & Co Ltd, 1981.

Collins, Larry R. and Page, Jr., James K. *Ling-Ling and Hsing-Hsing: Year of the Panda.* New York: Anchor Press/Doubleday, 1973.

Crammond, Joan. *The Giant Panda Book.* London: Paul Norbury Publications, 1974.

Eberle, Irmengarde. *Pandas Live Here.* New York: Doubleday & Company, Inc., 1973.

McClung, Robert M. *Lili, A Giant Panda of Sichuan.* New York: Morrow Junior Books, 1988.

McDearmon, Kay. *Giant Pandas.* New York: Dodd, Mead & Company, 1986.

Rogers, Barbara Radcliffe. *Giant Pandas.* New York: Mallard Press, 1990.

Wexo, John Bonnett. *Giant Pandas: Zoobooks series.* San Diego: Wildlife Education, Ltd., 1986.

Xuqi, Jin and Kappeler, Markus. *The Giant Panda.* New York: G.P. Putnam's Sons, 1986.

SEP - 1992